General George at Yorktown

a story in play form
by Carole Charles
pictures by Bob Seible

THE CHILD'S WORLD ELGIN, ILLINOIS 60120

The battle at Yorktown took place in October of 1781. It was the final great battle of the Revolutionary War.

Cornwallis was the commander of the British troops that occupied Yorktown. In late August, 1781, Cornwallis found American and French ships commanded by de Grasse to the northeast of Yorktown and Lafayette's troops to the south. By early October, Washington had arrived, commanding both French and American troops. Cornwallis was surrounded.

On October 9, Washington began bombarding Yorktown. The attempt to enter the city began on October 14. Cornwallis surrendered on October 19.

Even after this battle, though, the war dragged on. It was not over until April 19, 1783, exactly eight years after it had begun.

Library of Congress Cataloging in Publication Data

Charles, Carole, 1943-
 General George at Yorktown.

 (Stories of the Revolution)
 SUMMARY: A British drummer boy witnesses the last moments of the battle of Yorktown.
 1. Yorktown, Va.—Siege, 1781—Juvenile drama. [1. Yorktown, Va.—Siege, 1781—Drama. 2. United States—History—Revolution, 1775-1783—Drama. 3. Plays] I. Seible, Bob. II. Title.
PN6120.H5C47   812′.5′4   75-33158
ISBN 0-913778-23-0

Distributed by Childrens Press, 1224 West Van Buren Street, Chicago, Illinois 60607

General George
at Yorktown

(British soldiers and a drummer boy setting up tents in Yorktown.)

1st Soldier: Ha, ha! We've outsmarted the Americans again! Their band of ragged soldiers is no more than a nagging mosquito to the British army.

Drummer Boy: The Americans haven't much of an army, have they? But I hear General Washington is as good as a British general. Do you think we're safe here in Yorktown?

1st Soldier: Safe? Drummer boy, have you forgotten? We march with General Cornwallis. If Cornwallis says Yorktown is safe, then you can be sure Yorktown is safe!

Drummer Boy: I suppose. But the Chesapeake Bay isn't much protection without British ships.

1st Soldier: They'll be here if we need them, don't you worry. Now run off and help dig trenches. Not that we'll need much protection against that raggle-taggle American army!

(Yorktown, near British tents. Group of soldiers standing and sitting. Drummer boy enters running.)

Drummer Boy: Have you heard? Washington's troops might be heading this way!

2nd Soldier: Where did you hear that, lad?

Drummer Boy: A courier just arrived from New York. He says Washington's troops are on the march, perhaps to Yorktown!

2nd Soldier: Could be.

1st Soldier: And could be Washington wants us to think he's marching to Yorktown, so he can attack somewhere else, maybe even New York. Another American trick that won't fool anyone. Ha, ha!

Drummer Boy: But the courier said...

2nd Soldier: (interrupting) Relax, lad. If Washington did march on Yorktown, Cornwallis would have the whole British army and navy down here.

(British soldiers stand guard near the waters of Chesapeake Bay, just outside Yorktown.)

1st Soldier: Look there! A sail! It must be the British navy! Now what did I tell you? Didn't I say that Cornwallis would send for the whole British navy if...

2nd Soldier: *(interrupting)* Wait! That's not a British flag. It's *(straining to look)* ...it's a French flag!

1st Soldier: And another!

2nd Soldier: And another! Drummer boy, run up to the house General Cornwallis is using. Tell him there's a French fleet entering Chesapeake Bay. Hurry, lad!

(Inside British headquarters in Yorktown. Cornwallis paces. Secretary stands in background. Drummer boy stands watching Cornwallis.)

Cornwallis: How many French ships did you see?

Drummer Boy: I only saw three, sir, then ran to tell you. But there might be a whole fleet coming into...

Cornwallis: *(interrupting)* Yes, yes. *(Turns to secretary.)* Sergeant, take a count of the French ships. Then prepare a letter to be carried to New York immediately. Request British warships and all the land reinforcements New York can send. It looks as though the French navy has decided to help the Americans against us.

Drummer Boy: Do you think reinforcements will come in time, sir?

Cornwallis: *(distant, thoughtful)* I really don't know. Go along now, lad.

(Drummer boy and soldiers sit on a hill overlooking the Chesapeake Bay.)

Drummer Boy: *(excited)* Why don't our ships begin to fight the French? They're close enough. Why haven't they fired? The day will be gone before anything happens!

2nd Soldier: You don't want to hurry a battle too much, lad. It's like hurrying people to their death.

Drummer Boy: *(embarrassed)* Yes, sir.

1st Soldier: *(impatient)* What are our ships doing? They've given the French fleet nearly an hour and a half just to line up. *(exasperated)* Perhaps they're planning on dancing with each other instead of fighting a war. Come on! Fire!

(Distant boom of ship's cannon.)

Drummer Boy: They've fired!

1st Soldier: Ha, ha! You may depend upon it now, friends. The British navy will make kindling out of those fancy French ships. Go at it, men!

(Ship's cannon fires rapidly in the distance.)

(Drummer boy still watching battle from the same hill. Second soldier walks up to him.)

2nd Soldier: Are you still here, lad? I didn't think there'd be anything more to watch.

Drummer Boy: *(defeated)* I thought...maybe something would change. There were so many French ships. I counted 24. *(sigh)* Some of our ships look as though they're about to sink, don't they? Is there any hope for a new attack on the French?

2nd Soldier: Not this time, lad. Do you see? The British ships are beginning to go off to the north. They'll head up to New York and try to put themselves together again.

Drummer Boy: Have any reinforcements come from New York?

2nd Soldier: Not yet. But I hope they come soon. With the French in the bay, we'll need more help here in Yorktown.

Drummer Boy: *(agitated)* Why don't we move out? Couldn't we march to North Carolina?

2nd Soldier: Rumor says there are American troops out that way, and more marching down from the north.

Drummer Boy: That means Washington!

(Yorktown, inside a British soldier's tent. Second soldier sits on floor. First soldier runs into the tent, followed by drummer boy.)

1st Soldier: Washington's troops have marched into Williamsburg!

2nd Soldier: Ah, that's bad news. Williamsburg is only seven miles away. Now what will Cornwallis do?

1st Soldier: Cornwallis? What will I do? What will any of us do? We're caught like rats in a trap—the French in the bay, the Americans on land. And not one reinforcement has come from New York.

Drummer Boy: *(anguished)* What will happen to us?

(Soldiers and drummer boy digging trenches and construction redoubts outside Yorktown.)

1st Soldier: What a mistake Cornwallis has made this time. Have you seen the number of American and French troops out there? Washington must have 16,000 men. And that doesn't include a whole fleet of French ships in Chesapeake Bay. What do we have? Maybe 7,500 men? We don't stand a chance without reinforcements.

Drummer Boy: We at least have to try.

2nd Soldier: Now there's bravery for you. Just a boy, but he's willing to fight 16,000 Americans and French. *(gently)* For what, lad? For what?

Drummer Boy: For *(confused, thinking rapidly)* ...for England!

2nd Soldier: *(repeats quietly)* For England. But England is miles and miles across the sea. We're fighting a whole continent of people who just want to be left alone to farm their land, raise their children, make their own laws. If I lived in the colonies, I'd fight for that too.

(Two soldiers in a British redoubt outside Yorktown, just after midnight. All conversation is whispered.)

1st Soldier: I wonder how close the Americans are.

2nd Soldier: Probably close enough to hear us breathe.

1st Soldier: Well, you should be glad. You keep saying how much you'd like to see General Washington. This may be your chance.

(Branch cracks below.)

2nd Soldier: Who goes there?

Simpson: *(Speaks from ground, below the redoubt)* It's me, Simpson. General Cornwallis has ordered a retreat from all advance posts. You're to report back to Yorktown immediately!

2nd Soldier: So we're to give up the advance posts without a fight.

1st Soldier: We'll be giving up Yorktown next, unless reinforcements come from New York. Let's move out.

(British front line, about a mile from a redoubt newly occupied by the French and Americans. Two soldiers and drummer boy crouched down.)

1st Soldier: Keep an eye on that redoubt. I'd like a shot at a few American soldiers.

2nd Soldier: (thoughtfully, to himself)You'd only be killing fathers and brothers and sons.

1st Soldier: (angry) And what do you think they'll be killing when they start shooting at us? I'm a son too!

2nd Soldier: (to drummer boy) Lad, you keep an eye on the redoubt with that spyglass. I'm tired of fighting for something I no longer believe in. The Americans should have the right to make their own laws!

Drummer Boy: Look there! A group of Americans on horseback, right next to the redoubt! They look like officers.

1st Soldier: Ha, ha! Here's a cannon ball for the American officers!

(Two scenes on stage. British on one side. Washington on horseback, with aides, on other side. Cannon fires, flies over the heads of the Americans, lands near by.)

1st Soldier: Did we get them?

Drummer Boy: *(still looking through spyglass)* No, it went over their heads.

1st Soldier: Then we'll lower the cannon a bit. There! Fire!

(Cannon fires, lands beyond Washington's party, all the officers except Washington spur their horses to shelter.)

Drummer Boy: *(excited, laughing)* Boy! Did they run! Wait, there's one left. He's sitting on his horse, looking through his spyglass. He doesn't even seem afraid!

2nd Soldier: Let me see that glass. Ah, that must be General Washington himself. I hear he's not afraid of the whole British army.

Drummer Boy: Let me see!

1st Soldier: You saw already. Let me see. *(thoughtful)* George Washington. So that's the famous general.

2nd Soldier: Hey, you old soldier, I thought you wanted to keep firing that cannon.

1st Soldier: *(not hearing)* So that's General George Washington.

(Soldier and drummer boy beside tent 5:00 A.M.)

1st Soldier: *(intense, worried)* Tell me, what exactly did my friend say?

Drummer Boy: He said he couldn't go on fighting against the Americans. He walked across the lines with a white flag to give himself up.

1st Soldier: *(defeated)* If we're not dead, we'll soon be prisoners too.

(First cannon is fired on Yorktown.)

Drummer Boy: The firing has begun! Hurry!

1st Soldier: *(still defeated)* Hurry? For what? So I can die a little sooner?

(British hospital tent, crowded with casualties. First soldier lying on a pad on the floor with an injured leg. Continuous firing in background. Drummer boy, carrying water, approaches soldier.)

Drummer Boy: Here's water. *(hesitates)* How's your leg?

1st Soldier: *(listless)* All right. *(sits up halfway)* What's happening out there?

Drummer Boy: The firing hasn't stopped for a moment. This is the ninth day. I don't think... *(begins to break down).*

1st Soldier: *(impatient)* You don't think what?

Drummer Boy: I don't think we can hold out much longer. There aren't enough men left.

(Simpson enters tent.)

Simpson: Drummer boy! General Cornwallis wants to see you right away. Hurry up!

Drummer Boy: *(puzzled)* The General wants to see me? *(follows Simpson out)*

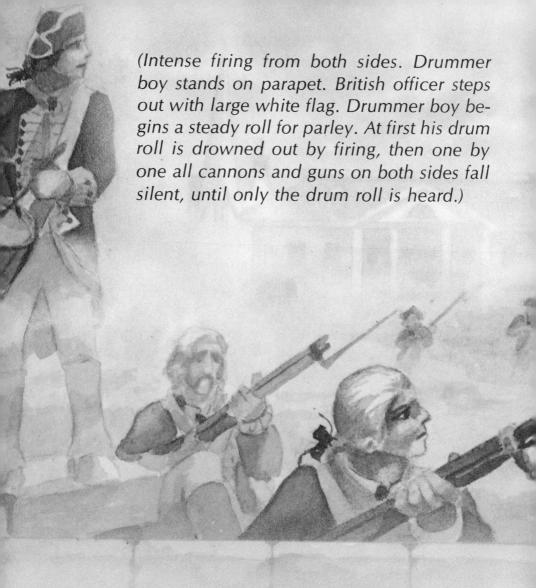

(Intense firing from both sides. Drummer boy stands on parapet. British officer steps out with large white flag. Drummer boy begins a steady roll for parley. At first his drum roll is drowned out by firing, then one by one all cannons and guns on both sides fall silent, until only the drum roll is heard.)

1st Soldier: (from offstage) It's over. General Washington has taken Yorktown. And with it he has taken the fight out of every British soldier.